Life on the Spectrum. The Preschool Years.

Getting the Help and Support You Need

By J.M. Worgan

(Trade paperback) ISBN-10: 1480026492

ISBN-13: 978-1480026490

(ebook) ASIN: B009JA2032

Contact the Author

Twitter; @mummyworgan

Facebook;
http://www.facebook.com/LifeOnTheSpectrumThePreschoolYears

Blog; www.goodreads.com/JMWorgan

www.glipho.com/JMWorgan

Dedication

For my father Stephen Allan Boden, 1950 – 1999. This book is for
you, my boys would have loved you Granddad.

Acknowledgements

If I have forgotten anyone I am truly sorry, but you know who you are.

Firstly my husband Andrew for all of his love and support. I am eternally thankful. You are a wonderful father to our two boys and my best friend. Thank you for putting up with me and my eccentricities for over twenty years.

Our respective parents. My mother Irene and step dad Peter for their constant support, understanding and words of wisdom and for making me laugh out loud. My in laws David and Sue for their support and encouragement and copious supplies of biscuits, juice and chocolate buttons. I never have to buy any.

Val, for her laughter and mad ways. You always make me smile. Thank you for the weekly phone calls.

To my lovely Nan who years ago gave me the best advice I have ever heard which was, 'don't listen to anyone, just do what you think is right'. My Nan is very wise.

Trisha, I will be eternally grateful for the help you gave Tom and to our family. Without you I dread to think were we would be now. You made a huge difference to the quality of our family life.

Lucy you are a true friend. You too gave us so much advice, support and most importantly understood what we were going through in those very early dark days. I will never forget your kindness.

Sarah your online Facebook community has truly helped and inspired me and one of the catalysts for writing this book. You are a wonderful mother, friend and autism advocate.

To all the mums, dads and friends I have made at AOK. Thank you.

Nippers Nursery staff. Thank you for helping to support Tom in those difficult early days, I will never forget how kind you were and for always seeing the positives in Tom.

Sara and Paula, thank you for all your kindness and hard work with Tom. We miss you too.

All the staff at Lune Park Children's Centre. You were like a second home to me, thank you for all your support.

Vince, thank you for the lovely book cover.

Unique Kidz and Co, thank you for your wonderful holiday club and allowing us some much needed respite time with Stephen.

Aukids magazine. Thank you Debby and Tori for such an informative and fun magazine.

The National Autistic Society who helped us in the early days and continue to help us today.

To all of the lovely parents I have chatted to online and been given advice and comfort, thank you.

Finally my two gorgeous boys. Thank you for all the joy and laughter you have brought into my life. Stephen, you are such a fantastic brother to Tom. We are very lucky to have such a kind and thoughtful (and imaginative) little boy. You are my little dinosaur explorer. Tom, thank you for just being you. You have allowed me to see the world in a totally new light. For that I am thankful. I love you both so very much.

Contents

Introduction

The Early Days before Help

Local Support and Services

'Bag of Tricks' and Sensory Issues

Help and Support on the Web

The Multidisciplinary Team

Siblings

Going Out and About

Toilet Training

In the Home

Education

Final Thoughts

Useful Information

I see autism as having many different strands. All of these strands are beautiful. They are all the colours of the rainbow intertwined intricately into the child. If you try and take away the autism by removing the strands you also take away parts of the child as they are attached to them. They are what make them who they are. However autism is only a part of them, not the whole. It does not define them.

J.M. Worgan

This is for my Tom

Introduction

Why did I decide to write this book? The simple reason is that I wanted to help families with newly diagnosed children on the autistic spectrum as well as children on their diagnostic journey who were of preschool age. The aim of this book is to help families through the difficult and emotional early years. My little boy is now four and he got his diagnosis of Autistic Spectrum Disorder (ASD) in the summer of 2011 when he was aged three. In both the period's pre and post diagnosis I was very lucky in that I got lots of support both emotionally and physically for myself, my husband Andrew, Tom and also for our other child Stephen who is sixteen months older. This was very important for all of us, so that we had knowledge and understanding in helping Tom with his difficulties and also so that Tom had access to early intervention and therefore the best possible start in life. Not everybody is as lucky to have such a wealth of help so early on so therefore I just want to share my story with you wherever you are on your diagnostic journey. You should be able to get the help and support that your family needs as well as being able to access the services that you need. This is to ensure the best possible start for your child so that they can reach their true potential and also so that you and your family are well supported. The best piece of advice I can give though is to have fun and a sense of humour. Enjoy your children; being on the spectrum is only part of them. See their diagnosis of autism as being a signpost rather than a description of who they are and what defines them. Don't get me wrong we have struggled and we have bad days but with support and a sense of humour you can get through anything and enjoy life.

The Early Days before Help

I just want to start by describing in a little detail what life was like with Tom before we got any help and intervention. As I have already mentioned every child is different and you will all have a very different story to tell. However this is my story and how life was like for me and my family. By giving you some of the details of what life were like with Tom in the early days it will help paint a picture of how life was. Maybe you will recognise and understand some of the problems as you may be experiencing them yourself. From this you can gain some comfort, you are not alone.

Tom was diagnosed in the summer of 2011 with Autistic Spectrum Disorder (ASD). He was diagnosed by a paediatric consultant at our local Child Development Centre, (CDC). This was on his fourth appointment. His first appointment was in January 2011.There will be more about the role of Child Development Centres and the role that they play later on. We noticed that Tom was 'different' around his first birthday. This was manifested in many different ways. He was hard to pacify and seemed to cry and become frustrated very easily. He would also shake his head backwards and forwards in an unusual movement, especially when frustrated. When eating we also noticed that he would roll his head in a circular movement. His speech and language also seemed to stop and not develop any further. From the age of one until around two we also saw other unusual behaviours develop which included, lack of eye contact, hand flapping, head rolling, pica(chewing though not swallowing non-food items), and having a very short attention span. He would also not do simple things such as wave or point at things. If he wanted something instead of pointing or asking for it he would take your hand and take you to what he wanted.

Daily life was becoming more and more difficult, especially as I had another child to look after. At this time I had to make a daily bus journey from our village to the local Children's Centre every morning. The journey itself only took ten minutes but I began to dread the mornings as the journey for Tom became more and more distressing and with it his behaviour more and more challenging. Once on the bus he would run into people, banging them with his head. He would also try and push people off a particular seat if that was where he wanted to sit. He would then refuse to sit on my knee and throw himself onto the floor and would then proceed to try and hide under the seats. As you can imagine it was a very stressful situation for both me and Tom. So as well as having to deal with this behaviour I had to look after a toddler while also struggling to carry a buggy on and off the bus. Looking back I can now smile and even laugh as it seems such a long time ago but at the time I just felt like throwing myself onto the floor and joining him.

We now know though with hindsight that Tom was having great difficulties in dealing with all of the sensory information that he was trying to process. He also could not cope with getting onto a crowded bus. There will be more about sensory issues and the difficulties that children with autism face later on as we now know more about how children on the autistic spectrum show problems in dealing with sensory processing, including hypo and hyper sensitivities. Tom is hypersensitive to loud noises and hyposensitive to touch in that he craves this type of tactile sensory stimulation. On a positive note though by the time that Stephen had finished nursery and we no longer needed to get the bus, most of the passengers knew about Tom and his difficulties and tried to help. One lovely lady used to give me her assortment of key rings for Tom to play with, which he enjoyed immensely. We certainly livened up the journey every morning! Wonder if they miss us?

Tom did exhibit (and still does to a lesser degree) challenging behaviour. He would run into people using his head, usually in busy places and especially when waiting outside the nursery reception area. He would also throw objects when distressed. One particular thing he did that really frightened me was to head-butt glass, mainly windows and the television. At the time this was happening I sought lots of help for ways in which I could stop him from doing this as I was petrified that he would seriously hurt himself. The general consensus though from the professionals involved was that he would know how much pressure to exert and that over time if ignored (which was very hard for a parent to do) he would eventually stop. Luckily this did happen, over a period of a few months the episodes became less frequent until one day we noticed that he had not 'head banged' for over a week.

Change and the need for sameness also made itself known around this time. When out in town pushing him in his buggy he made it perfectly clear by shouting and trying to push the buggy with his body which way he wanted to go. I soon realised that he wanted to go the same route every time. This was fairly easy when going into town as there was only really one way to walk but we had a choice of two bridges to cross. Things were a little more difficult in the shopping precinct as I would have to use the same route every time. This somewhat limited my choice of shops!

One thing he found difficult when out and about shopping was being in busy and crowded shops and cafes. I would take him to the coffee shop but it would always be before ten o'clock in the morning and he would eat his usual pack of wafers and have the same drink. This is something that he still enjoys doing today! Tom also found the supermarket particularly difficult so I therefore found it easier to go very early and have a prepared list with me so that we could do the shopping as quickly as possible. His 'bag of tricks' as I liked to call them was always readily available and attached to the back of the buggy.

Tom was also showing difficulties regarding his speech and language. He would grab my hand and take me to what he wanted rather than to ask or say the word. This improved over time as I would make him say the word before I would walk with him, a strategy that over time worked really well. We could also tell that he did not understand things fully and that he did not respond to his name when called or when giving simple instructions. It was as if he did not hear us.

He also stopped eating certain foods, something that had not been a problem when weaning as he would eat anything given to him. He started to want the same foods all of the time and he preferred 'dry' foods to 'wet' foods. He would also not progress onto new foods. He had problems with his bowels; they were very loose and foul smelling. He would pass at least four loose stools a day. The problems with diet, eating and toileting will all be discussed in further chapters.

I only want this introduction to describe how life was for my family in the early days, in the days before we got help. I was very fortunate in that Andrew was very supportive. We both knew that Tom was having problems and we were in agreement that Tom would need professional help. I am very lucky in that Andrew is a fantastic father to both my sons and he is particularly patient and understanding of Tom. Andrew coped fantastically well with Tom's behaviour and would take him out for me, going for a drive in the car or for a walk about to give me a break. He would also have both boys for a whole day at the weekend if I had worked a night shift (I was working as a nurse at the time doing one night shift a week). Andrew went and still goes to a local Dads Club group at the local Children's Centre and although the group is for all children, not specifically for children with additional needs, he has made lots of friends and is able to chat to the other fathers there about Tom as they all know about his difficulties and are very understanding. I am also very fortunate with my little boy Stephen. He understands Tom very well, is very supportive of him and is forever telling everyone that he is his 'best friend'. He is such a caring and understanding little boy.

What I really want to focus on is all the support, information and help that I did get for our family so that we were better enabled and prepared to care for Tom as well as Tom himself receiving specialist care tailored to meet his needs. It was so important that we received all of these early interventions and advice from professionals and friends as they helped make a tremendous difference to our quality of life. Most importantly life got more enjoyable

Local Support and Services

We first received support for Tom from our local Children's Centre. They help families with children under the age of five. They run groups, courses such as healthy eating and positive parenting, run baby clinics, baby massage and may run groups for children with additional needs. The group for children with additional needs, (AOK) at our local Children's Centre was our saving grace. We were put in touch with the special needs outreach worker who supported the group and we started going there once a week, myself Tom and Stephen. We have now been going to the group on and off for over two years and have made many friends.

Tom was known to the Children's Centre staff as he was already in nursery there for two mornings a week. It was while at nursery that his difficulties and challenging behaviour was 'picked up' by nursery staff and the early years teacher. I always remember the day when I was approached by nursery staff when Tom had only been in nursery a few months asking if I could have a meeting with them to discuss his progress as he was struggling. I felt as if a huge weight had been lifted from me, at last somebody acknowledged that there was a problem. It was at this meeting that we decided to refer Tom to the Child Development Centre (CDC) so that they could assess him. Therefore I will discuss in a little detail what a CDC is and what services they offer. I certainly did not know what they were or that they even existed before entering the world of autism.

When I first heard about the CDC I had no idea what would happen there. I had a mixture of emotions, I was happy that Tom would be receiving help but I did not like the unknown and uncertainty of what would happen. Both Andrew and I knew long before his referral that something was 'not right' but it was hard to act upon as we did not know what to do, who to go to or how to put into words what exactly was wrong, even though we knew that he needed professional help. I imagine that this is what it must feel like for most parents whose children are having difficulties at such a young age. We both hoped that once he started nursery we would get professional help and luckily we did.

Basically a CDC is part of the NHS. A child will be referred as there are problems with their development, that they are not developing as a child of their age normally does and that they are not meeting their developmental milestones. A child can be referred by a GP, health visitor, Special Educational Needs Coordinator or indeed any social care provider. Our lovely health visitor made our referral. The CDC is where many different professional are based. These include consultant paediatricians, occupational therapist (OT), speech and language therapists (SALT) and clinical psychologists, Therefore there is a whole team of professionals who can help assess the child and can then give specialised help and care.

I did not know what to expect on our first appointment. However during this time in my life I was very well supported. I had been put in touch with the support group, an outreach worker (who specialised in special needs) had been assigned to me and I had made contact with other parent carers of children on the spectrum. Therefore I had a strong support network and I feel that this is the most important thing when caring for a child with any additional needs. I did not feel alone. I urge anyone reading this now that has a child who is having problems and difficulties to go out and visit your local Children's Centre if you are fortunate enough to have one in your local area. They have a wealth of knowledge and support to offer you.

To prepare myself for the visit a specialist health visitor made a home visit prior to the clinic appointment. She came to our house and had a chat with Andrew and me while observing Tom playing. She also asked some questions about his development and what we thought his problems were. It was very informal and unthreatening. She explained that all of the information she gathered would be given to the paediatrician in preparation for our clinic appointment. She also informed us that she would be present at the appointment. This made me less anxious as she would be a friendly face who had met Tom. I was also very lucky in that my outreach worker came with me for support during the initial appointment so that she could help settle Tom while I could discuss my worries and concerns with the paediatrician. I still remember that first appointment and the mixture of emotions I had. Tom did not cope very well and tried to escape from the room several times; he also threw objects and was hitting out at people. It was his way of telling us that he was not happy and that he could not cope with the new surroundings and situation. It was very distressing for Tom and for me too as an observer. At least on a positive note the doctor saw him as his 'real self', that I was thankful for. I was told at this appointment that Tom was possibly on the autistic spectrum due to his delayed speech and language and problems with social communication and interaction but that he was too young for a definitive diagnosis. Although I knew that he was probably on the spectrum (I had done my research and followed my gut instinct) it was still a shock to hear it out loud. No matter how thankful I was to hear it.

During these very early years I found that support from other parents really helped me in that they helped me to stay grounded, stay positive, that it was ok to feel frightened and anxious about the future as well as having feelings of frustration and anger and fleetingly that I somehow was to blame. Indeed that it was normal to have all of these mixed up emotions. In a sense going through the diagnostic process and being informed that your child has a disability is very much a learning process in that you first have to accept that your child has a disability before you can then move on and be able to help your child. You have to move through the five stages of loss (denial, anger, bargaining, depression and acceptance) as defined by Kubler-Ross (1973), in order to achieve this. It is almost as if the journey you had planned for your child is totally changed and that the future becomes less clear.

My new found friends were also fantastic for having a laugh with but most importantly they understood. They had been through the whole journey themselves. As I have already mentioned AOK in a way saved my life and my family and I will be eternally grateful to the parents and staff who ran and still run the group today. It is a place where Tom can play with his peers (and Stephen too in the holidays) and I can have a chat to other mums. This is something that cannot be achieved at 'normal' toddler and baby groups, I tried! I persevered for so long at these groups but to be honest it was a total nightmare. I had to keep a constant eye on Tom as I was not sure how he would react with the other children and I could not sit and chat to the other mums as I was too preoccupied to do so. I also used to get 'those stares' as his behaviour would be perceived to be odd. The whole toddler group experience was sadly not a good one with Tom, something that I still feel badly about as I really enjoyed the toddler group circuit with Stephen. This is why the support group was so much needed. Everybody understood about Tom and his needs. Nobody judged us and for any parent this is what matters most I think. The group was also a fantastic way to find out information locally. I should also mention at this point that I got a lot of support from the parent representative who helped run and still runs the group today. She herself has a child with Asperger's Syndrome as well as two other younger children. Her support, friendship and knowledge really helped me to adjust to my new way of life and I will be eternally grateful to her.

As well as the support group at the Children's Centre there is also a group once a month at another local Children's Centre, especially for parent carers of children and young people on the autistic spectrum. This aspect of being labelled a parent carer at first I found to be very difficult. How could I be a carer for my own child? Surely this is what every parent does? But once having spoken to other parents of children with ASD I soon began to realise that caring for a child on the spectrum was much more complex than caring for a child not on the spectrum due to them having additional needs. I soon realised this by comparing my two boys, which I know you shouldn't do, but I did anyway. Being a parent carer and the additional stress, time and sheer energy needed to look after your child does mean that you are a parent carer and that you are entitled to additional support and benefits including Disability Living Allowance (DLA) and Carer's Allowance. You could contact your local child and family support officer based at your local county council for help and advice regarding benefits that parent carers are entitled to.

At the parent carer support group carers would meet once a month to chat and find out information related to ASD and the role of being a carer. The group although mainly for parents would welcome preschool children along to play. I did take Tom along a few times but for reasons I did not and still do not understand he did not like it there and would become distressed. Therefore I only went twice but I will hopefully go more often once Tom is in school full time. The group also has a resource library in which you can borrow books relating to ASD. This I found extremely valuable.

Therefore you should not feel alone and isolate yourself. This is something that is very easy to do and sometimes if you are having a particularly challenging day where your child is in their room for time outs every ten minutes (I have had those days) then it is extremely easy to shut yourself away as it takes extra energy and willpower to actually make it out of the house to meet people without crying. I am glad I made the effort though as meeting other likeminded parents really helped me. I soon realised that there are other parents out there with autistic children and that they are having the same daily challenges as I am.

I also want to mention in this chapter about holiday clubs for respite care. Our local club 'Unique Kidz' is run in the school holidays and they have an after school club as well. The club provides activities in a secure and safe setting were children receive specialist care to meet their additional needs while playing and having fun. The club is for children and young people with disabilities. We very much need this service as a family. It gives Tom the chance to socialise with his peers in a safe setting. We never worry about him when he is there as we know he is well looked after. It also gives Andrew, Stephen and I time to have a break together. This is a very rare occurrence for us as we have nobody living locally who could spend time with Tom. So on the occasions when Tom is at Unique Kidz we go out and have fun for the six hours that he is there. We go out and eat lunch, something that is not possible for us as a family at the moment as Tom will not sit still for long enough. We also go out to places which would be difficult for Tom such as busy cafes and explore new places. If you contact your local county council you should be able to find information about local holiday clubs and short breaks for children with additional needs and disabilities.

It is also of importance to mention in this chapter that local parent carer forums are really useful for keeping updated and informed about developments locally and nationally. For example you will find information about short breaks, respite and overnight respite care, local schemes such as Peace of Mind (a carers service were in the case of an emergency there is a plan in place for a carer to sit and look after your child) and changes to government policy regarding Special Educational Needs (SEN). It is also a place where your opinions can be heard. As well as finding out about services and provision locally you can also have input into what services you would like to access for your child. More importantly it is also a great place to meet like-minded parents.

I should also mention the importance of support from family members, including the extended family. It is important that you get emotional and physical support in your caring role. I know from experience that for a lot of parent carers this is not the case. Both of our respective parents live in the same area, seventy miles away, so although we do not get the daily physical support what is more important I feel is that we do get emotional support. This is vital I feel to your mental health and wellbeing, to know that you are supported by loved ones and not being judged is extremely valuable. For family to understand that your child's behaviour is actually caused by a developmental disability and not bad patenting is what most parents want their family to acknowledge. I feel very fortunate that this is the case.

The general point I am trying to get across here is that you need to find out what services and groups are in your local area. Go and find information on your local county council website and search for local support groups, contact your local Children's Centre, phone up the local council. Help is out there but sometimes you just need to go out and find it.

'Bag of Tricks' and Sensory Issues.

When starting to write this chapter I initially wanted to discuss sensory issues separately but once I started to write about Tom's 'bag of tricks' I soon came to the conclusion that I needed to discuss them as a whole as the items in the bag were used to help Tom with his sensory needs for a variety of reasons

Firstly I need to discuss Tom's sensory needs. Many children on the autistic spectrum have difficulty processing sensory information and may be hypersensitive (under sensitive to stimuli) hyposensitive to sensory stimuli (oversensitive) and even both hypo and hypersensitive. For example Tom is hypersensitive to noise on the busy road and the vacuum cleaner but hyposensitive to touch. Many children on the autistic spectrum have difficulties in processing sensory information from the environment around them. The ways in which children can demonstrate that they are craving sensory stimulation can be by, crashing into objects, running, jumping and touching people repeatedly. This is very typical of Tom's behaviour.

When we started receiving help and support from the Children's Centre for Tom it soon became apparent that Tom was seeking sensory stimulation through touch and that he was demonstrating this in a number of ways. Firstly he would run into people with his head, his head would therefore be the first point of contact. He would also use his head to bang on windows and the television. Thankfully this has now stopped. He would also throw himself at objects such as tables, especially if things were on them as in the nursery he attended. It was almost as if he was finding his own way of releasing his tension and feelings of frustration allowing him when once released to relax. Once he had he would then calm down and would find being stroked on the back, arms, hands and head very relaxing. He would calm down very quickly. This was a strategy used by nursery staff and it proved to be very effective. He would lie on textured cushions while the staff moved his hand over the cushion. He would enjoy the sensory sensation. We still do this at home today. He loves to lie snuggled up surrounded by his cushions, he calls it 'hide and seek'.

My outreach worker helped me to find and develop strategies that would help with his sensory needs at home. We were very lucky as the Children's Centre have a sensory room and myself and Tom would access this once a week during the support group and use it with other children as well as accessing the room privately once a week with myself as it would be booked in advance. I used to enjoy this hour long session very much as I used to play calming music and we would often lie on the bean bag and look at all the different lights and colours, it was a very relaxing atmosphere to be in. We would also on occasions use the room before nursery started if Tom was particularly distressed after his bus journey. Some days were better than others. The sensory room became a safe haven for Tom. It had bubble tubes, a light wall, fibre optic lights, an interactive play wall and lots of different sensory toys such as sensory balls, fabrics, musical instruments and cushions etc. I was very fortunate in that I could try out and borrow sensory equipment at home. Therefore we could find out what worked for Tom. Specialist sensory toys can be very expensive to buy but there are schemes out there were you can lend equipment. One good example is that Cerebra, a charity for children with neurological problems, has a sensory toy lending library service were you can borrow such items as sensory tubs, bubble tubes and fibre optic lights. You can borrow one item for twenty eight days and it is a free service. This is a good way to 'test drive' toys before you buy them.

We were very fortunate in that we were able to borrow a bubble tube and fibre optic lights from the Children's Centre. Tom loved them initially. They really helped to calm him when frustrated or overstimulated. However after six months they started to lose their use as Tom became disinterested. It is important to note that the child may become 'used' to a certain toy after a period of time and it may lose its therapeutic use. Therefore other toys and strategies can be tried; this is what we do constantly with Tom. What he really liked and what he still uses today is a vibrating snake. This is a plastic tube which is in the shape of the letter C and when switched on at the end vibrates very gently. This really helps to calm Tom. He often lies on the floor with it on his back or puts it around his neck. It was also very useful in the early days at nursery as it helped to get him into the room as well as calming him once in there.

So what was in my 'bag of tricks'? Well it did change from week to week so as to keep Tom interested but it always contained the following. A toy car, Tom was and still is fixated with cars or indeed anything with wheels. Sometimes I would put in a toy train from home. The car would always be a cheap £1 car so that if he dropped it on the bus or threw it into the canal it could be easily replaced. However one day I made the fatal mistake of buying a cheap car from the local supermarket when he was with me. Ever since then the supermarket has been called the 'car shop'. I now need to buy a car before doing the shopping every time we visit the shop together. Is this bad patenting? Maybe, but at least I have a relatively calm shopping experience now. What is interesting though is that if Andrew takes him shopping to the same supermarket he will not ask for a car.

Tom when going through his phase of throwing things in the canal once threw in his toy bird (the kind which you find in gift shops at local wildlife centres which when pressed tweet at you.) Perhaps he thought it would swim and meet his friends! We always had a bird in his bag but I was always careful to hide it when on the canal. However many times his bird was left behind on the bus for us to collect at the Lost Property Office and once his Robin had a lovely day out to Kendal on the bus. It was returned to us later on that day on the return journey, all thanks to a lovely friendly lady at the Lost Property Office. He still loves his toy birds today, we have around six of them and he often lies with them on the floor surrounded by his cushions pretending they are flying while chatting to them.

I always had a book in the bag; his favourite for a long time was 'The Gingerbread Man', He also enjoyed any books with cars and trains in them. Books were really useful when Tom was sitting in his buggy as we would happily sit there looking at the pictures. What was always in his bag was the trusted Nintendo DS. This really helped when in the supermarket as it would very easily distract him as well as being very light, small and easy to carry about. It was a lifesaver when sitting in the coffee shop, it would keep him entertained. I also used to have a wad of paper and felt tips in the bag for when in a cafe. He would happily sit and scribble on about twenty sheets of paper. I found one of his jotter pads from our early cafe days the other day. The drawings evoked such early memories. Shakers were also a favourite of Tom's, we had a cheap pair at home and these were ideal for taking out. Another firm favourite was the squashy ball, the type that is textured and when you squash parts of it they pop out. We had these particular toys in the shape of balls and caterpillars and Tom would simply feel them with his hands and put them on his face. He still does this today. I also on some occasions used to put pieces of train track in the bag so that if we were in a cafe or coffee shop he could push the train up and down. It is really strange to think back in time to how I used to rely on my' bag of tricks', it used to go with Tom everywhere,

We still rely very heavily on sensory toys at home. We use them to help calm him down when frustrated and upset. We also use them therapeutically in that we massage him with the sensory ball on his back, face, arms and legs. We have a box in the lounge which contains all of the toys so that Tom can go and get them when needed. We have at this moment in his box the following. Sensory balls, flashing tambourine, bendy man, cosmic spinner, small hand bells, large sensory ball, feathers, slinky, rubbery sensory ball, bouncing flashing ball, flashing bracelet and sensory octopus squishy toy. We also have a large sensory mat made of soft fabric. Tom loves to lie stretched out on this. What Tom really enjoys as does Stephen and myself is making a sensory den. You can buy sensory dens but they are extremely expensive so I make do with 'do it yourself'. I simply drape a large emergency foil blanket over two chairs to make the den (these are extremely cheap), put a rug underneath and then place the toys in the den. It is a lovely dark place to play in and looks especially soothing when we have all the toys lit up in it. The boys have hours of fun playing in it. We were very fortunate in that we received help from The

Family Fund, in which we were able to buy the sensory items. We were also able to buy other items such as a beanbag which is very good, Tom often takes himself off and will sit on it in his book corner to have a bit of time out. He also lies on his mat and places the beanbag on his back; he must like the feeling of pressure and maybe he feels more secure. It looks very funny though! We also have magnetic letters and a magnetic board but Tom prefers to put the letters on the floor, scattering them about always in the same place. Play dough and play foam are also firm favourites in our house. Play dough is fantastic for children who seek out sensory stimulation. Homemade is best I feel as it is cheap to make. You can make lots of colours and if put in the mouth you know it is safe. Tom has only recently stopped putting things in his mouth; he now touches things to his lips. It was a great concern at the time though as I would be constantly worried about him choking on small objects. He would also chew his cuffs and bite on objects. We found out over time that he was doing this to gain pleasure through his senses, it felt nice to him. So at the time that this was happening I found out if there was anything I could buy for him to chew on to replace him biting his clothing and other objects. This was by asking my lovely network of mum friends and using the Internet. In my search I read many recommendations about 'chew stixx'. We had two of them, one in the shape of a stick and the other a cross. Tom absolutely loved them and they survived his constant chewing for over a year. A bonus was that they were also relatively inexpensive. There are lots on the market and some of my clever friends attach them to ribbons so that they cannot be lost. You can also get chewy necklaces and other chewable toys.

So from all of this information it was very clear that Tom was and still is seeking out sensory stimulation, particularly to touch. At the beginning of our journey to find out why Tom was exhibiting certain behaviours such as head butting and pica we were very fortunate in that myself and Andrew were able to have two appointments with a clinical psychologist. We wanted to gain ideas and strategies in which we could help Tom with regards to his challenging behaviour. The role of the clinical psychologist is to work with the child in order to help reduce anxiety and to promote well-being. We described all of Tom's behaviours and what we were concerned with and it became clear that he was seeking out sensory situations and that he was hyposensitive to touch. This was when we were given ideas and strategies to use as well as a list of good books on the subject. The use of sensory toys, touch, deep massage and rough and tumble play were also discussed. Tom at the time was very energetic; he would run up and down a room all day and would be constantly jumping off the couches. It was explained to us that Tom was doing this kind of movement again to get the feelings he needed; he could not get them by merely walking. It was then that a trampoline was suggested as a way for Tom to get the sensory stimulation he needed and also a way for him to burn energy off and find the release he needed, a similar feeling he was getting by using his head to run at people and hit the television. We were very fortunate in that our father in law bought us a trampoline but there are grants out there to help families with disabled children to be able to buy one. The trampoline has become a very much needed piece of equipment, no matter the weather! I heartily recommend one, even if you don't have a large space in your garden you could buy a small trampoline for one child with a bar that they hold onto. This will be just as effective.

I also feel that it is important that soft play areas are discussed. We go to several locally and although very good we usually go when we know it is going to be fairly quiet. I particularly like going around lunch time for this reason. I am always on tender hooks though and feel that I have to keep a constant eye on Tom and what he is up to. However recently there has been the emergence of multi-sensory specialist soft play centres around the country especially for disabled children. We were very fortunate in that we were able to take both Tom and Stephen to 'Boomerang' a multi-sensory play centre in Bury which Is apparently the largest multi-sensory play area open to all children in the north west area. It was fantastic! There was a sensory room, soft play room, interactive room and a cafe! All in a safe and secure environment, we didn't need to worry about Tom escaping! I would highly recommend it. The fantastic thing was that Stephen could play there too and be included, something of great importance. I would definitely find your local specialist play centre and give it a go.

So to conclude I feel that you have to find out what sensory needs your child has, through asking professionals and observing your child yourself, you know them best. Find books on the subject, ask friends, look for websites and then think of ways in which you can help your child by including a sensory diet into their everyday activities. You could use play dough, play with cars in sand, use water, play with pasta shapes and make a snow storm shaker in a plastic bottle. Could you make up a small bag of toys or make a corner of a room into a sensory den? The opportunities are endless and it needn't cost a lot of money. You will have fun at the same time too.

Help and Support on the web

Having support locally is very important and nothing can compare to having physical friends who can actually give you a hug and that so much needed physical contact. However help and support can also be gained in the virtual world through a variety of resources. I will comment upon websites and web pages that I have used and still use to gain information about ASD,all the topics related to ASD, and all of the lovely people I have met and who have become friends. There is so much support out there.

The National Autistic Society (NAS) was the first major website that i want to introduce you to. They are the country's leading charity for adults and children who are on the autistic spectrum, their parents, carers and professionals. They provide information, support and services as well as doing fabulous campaign work to educate and inform the public about autism and related conditions. This was the first website I accessed when I first became concerned about Tom and it was the first website I went too once we received a diagnosis. There is an absolute wealth of information relating to young children on the spectrum ranging from dietary needs to potty training. There is also lots of practical help, advice sheets, useful references and details of courses and training. It also updates you on research and government policy. I have accessed the website many times over the past couple of years. At first I wanted to find out general information regarding ASD and then later on our journey to find out about sensory issues and toilet training. I gained a lot of insight by doing so. Recently I looked at their education section and in particular getting the help and support for your child at school. What is really important though is that there is a whole section on the website dedicated to being a patent, carer or relative of an autistic child. What I particularly find useful is their dedicated support pages for helping grandparents and siblings of autistic children. These have helped me and my family tremendously. What I find really useful though is that they have a community forum which you can join. This is for people on the autistic spectrum as well as parents, carers and relatives. Once you have registered and you have made your profile, which is very easy to do you can then access the online community and start to make your own posts. There is a specific forum related to being a parent carer of an autistic child which I have found very useful. You find that you are talking to likeminded people who offer you practical help and advice from their own experiences. However there is also a lighter side as you can also have discussions about hobbies and everyday life. The main thing is it gets you connected to parents who are in a similar position as yourself. Another wonderful resource that the NAS offer is their e befriending service. This is where you can request a volunteer e befriended who will communicate with you via email. You determine how often you would like to communicate. They also pair you up with a person who has been in a similar situation to yourself and who shares your common interests. It is a wonderful scheme. You can apply by downloading their application form. I should also mention that there is a support helpline which is free and confidential. You can phone and discuss any problems related to autism and caring for your autistic child. By becoming a member of the NAS you receive wonderful benefits such as a quarterly magazine, newsletters, and discounts off conferences and NAS publications.

ASD Friendly is another wonderful forum. This is a very friendly site that was set up in 2003. There is a community forum as well as live chats throughout the week. I have had lots of useful advice given from this site. It is well worth visiting.

Facebook, well I just have to mention social networking and in particular Facebook. This is an excellent way to communicate with parents who live locally and who you know personally as well as meeting in the virtual world other parents and carers who live further afield, who have children on the spectrum. There are lots of groups dedicated to the families and carers of children who are on the autistic spectrum as well as support groups dedicated to parents of children with any disability. I have met many good friends this way. The support that you get can be truly overwhelming. You are able to chat about any issues or concerns you have or indeed you can be a silent member and gain support and advice that way. It is worth doing a search yourself and finding out what groups are near you.

I have only just recently found out about Cerebra and the wonderful services that they offer. Cerebra are a charity that helps children and their carers with neurological problems including autism. Their services include a toy lending library as discussed in the previous chapter, a postal book lending library, advice about grants, help with Disability Living Allowance, (DLA) and other disability rights, personal rights, a personal portfolio making service, they run a stress helpline and also have publications on managing stress as a carer as well as a quarterly magazine for members entitled Newsbeat. Membership to Cerebra is free. I will discuss the postal book lending library and portfolio services as I have used them fairly recently in more detail. I have borrowed many books from the postal books lending library. You have to register as a member to be able to use the service, but as mentioned membership is free. You are allowed to borrow two books at any one time for up to twenty eight days; this may be extended if nobody else has requested them. There are publications on many aspects of ASD, including behaviour, education, sensory issues and toileting difficulties. It is a wonderful service and I urge you to have a look at what is available. I have also used their personal portfolio service. This is sometimes called a passport or personal profile. Basically it is a book that you can give to anyone who looks after your child so that they can better understand and communicate with them. The portfolio will include an introduction about your child and family, what the child likes and dislikes, favourite activities, why the child is different, how you can help the child, important information, school, their life journey, who supports them, contact information and a photo gallery. How is this created? You download and print off their booklet which you then fill in. The more information and details you give them the better. You then send it back to them at their Freepost address. You can post photographs with the booklet or you can send them separately by email. I emailed mine separately. I received Tom's personal portfolio a few weeks ago and was very happy with the finished product. It contains all of the information that anybody new to meeting Tom would need. It will be particularly useful for Tom's Reception class teacher and teaching assistant when starting school.

Your local library is well worth investigating. From personal experience, going to the library and browsing the shelves for particular books of interest is not a practical option when you have a small child with you. Therefore I always use the online library catalogue to search and order books. There is usually a small charge for this service, I have to pay sixty pence per reservation, but the positives far outweigh this negative. You can search for a particular book, do broad subjects search and you are able to search from all libraries in the county giving you greater choice. I also reserve novels, much cheaper than buying them!

Disabled Living is a charity which provides services, information and equipment for disabled adults and children. They also have a helpline. I have found the website to be very useful. They have a supplier directory that lists products that may help your child. These are divided into different areas of the house and garden so that you can pin point your needs. For example they give details of a company who can help you design a sensory space in your home or garden. There are lots of fabulous ideas. The website also gives information and a link to PromoCon; this is a national service which provides information and help regarding bladder and bowel continence for both adults and children. In particular they have information sheets and publications on toilet training for children with special needs. I have accessed these publications and have found them to be very useful. (I am still in the process of toilet training Tom). There is also a helpline staffed by qualified continence nurses. I have phoned several times for advice and always feel reassured and have been given excellent advice.

I also want to lastly mention that they have a 'Kidz' page in which they give details about their Kidz exhibitions. There are three events a year, Kidz up North, Kidz in the Middle and Kidz South. They are the UK's largest free exhibitions that are for children with disabilities, additional needs, parents, carers and professionals. I have been fortunate enough to go to two exhibitions over the past two years and I was very impressed with the amount of information I received regarding autism and related difficulties. It is also a fun place to be, the freebies you get are fantastic. I heartily recommend a visit; it won't cost you a penny.

Aukids is a positive parenting quarterly magazine which is produced by Debby Elley, mum and journalist of twin boys who have autism and Tori Houghton, a speech and language therapist. Their excellent magazine contains lots of fun advice, practical tips, and reviews of books relating to ASD's and apps for parents who have young children on the autistic spectrum. Their website also contains lots of useful information especially if your child is newly diagnosed or if you are at the beginning of gaining a diagnosis. You can try a sample copy of the magazine via their website and there is an excellent starter's special which is available to subscribers and support groups. It is well worth taking a look at the website. To sum up here is their ethos 'Why can't I have a coffee table read that I enjoy whilst I'm learning to help my child? That was the question that influenced us as we set about considering the style and tone of the magazine. Special needs and a sense of humour are rarely paired up in publications – why not? Our readers, who are parents and teachers working with autistic children, feel less isolated and more positive because of the magazine's positive tone'. This is a sentiment that I whole heartily share.

SEN Assist is a company which makes specialist CD-ROMs for autistic children both at school and at home. The company is run by a husband and wife team, this is a quote taken from Adele on the SEN Assist Blog "I'm a special needs teacher at an autism specific school in Surrey. England. I have over a decade of experience helping children with autism play and learn. My training includes TEACCH, Pecs, Intensive interaction and social stories. I co-founded the award winning SEN Assist with my husband Quentin in 2010.Together we create software and resources to help ALL children learn." i first found out about this wonderful service over a year ago. I was searching for Christmas presents for Tom and was recommended to look at the website by a friend. I was so excited by what I found. They have six CD-ROMs for sale all based on children's nursery rhymes and stories including 'Little Red Riding Hood' and 'The Gingerbread Man'. The beauty of the website is that you can try out the software before you buy. Tom tried 'The Gingerbread Man' and it was an instant hit. You can also download 'Little Red Riding Hood' for free. Each CD -ROM is an interactive story book including twenty four activities and comes with printable resources of the story. Tom finds the software easy to use, as using the mouse requires a 'click' and 'click' movement rather than a 'drop' and 'drag'. This causes less frustration and episodes of anger. The website itself also has lots of free resources including Christmas story activities and a matching card activity. The SEN Blog is also excellent, giving support and practical advice to parents of autistic children. I urge you to take a look.

There is also one other online community I want to mention. Talk About Autism is a national charity for children and young people with autism. They provide a community where you can discuss all topics related to ASD as a parent carer. They also offer as well as the community forum a question and answer service; you have access to previous sessions as well as details of forthcoming ones. Other benefits include an information links library, advice on transitions, information regarding newly diagnosed children, education and oral health.

The main point I want to convey is that there is an abundance of help and information out there on the Internet. There is however a lot of misinformation out there and some terrible websites but if you go to registered charity websites and recommended websites and forums you will gain a lot of useful information and help. You may also meet some new friends along the way.

The Multidisciplinary Team

When you are at the beginning of your diagnostic journey with your child you soon realise that there is not just one professional who will be helping your family and diagnosing your child. The help you receive is from a multidisciplinary team and the diagnosis from the collected thoughts, observations and knowledge from all of the care givers working with yourself and your child. This has been my experience and I want to share it with you. Others will have a different story but by telling mine it may perhaps make the whole process seem less daunting and that in the end you get the help that you so desperately need. It may also help explain the process of gaining a diagnosis for your child although as I have already stated you may have a totally different experience.

There have been many professionals involved in the care and assessment process for Tom. They include the consultant paediatrician, occupational therapist (OT), early year's speech and language therapist (SALT), clinical psychologist and paediatric dietician. I will not talk about the professionals involved with education such as Portage and educational psychologists as I will discuss these professionals in the chapter regarding education.

Our first step on the diagnostic ladder was with the consultant paediatrician, this is the doctor who is responsible for the diagnosis, treatment and overall care of the child. We had four appointments in total over the course of a year which resulted in Tom's diagnosis of ASD. I felt and still feel very much supported by our paediatrician, In particular I was given lots of information very early on including details of local patent support groups and a parental booklet entitled 'Information for Parents. Autistic Spectrum Disorders (ASD's) and related conditions.'(2010). It was very difficult at first for her to give a definitive diagnosis of ASD as Tom was very young as he was only two and a half years of age. His challenging behaviour could have been as a result from his difficulties with speech and language, in that he was showing his distress physically. However over the course of the year it became clearer that Tom was on the autistic spectrum and this was through observing Tom in clinic, asking myself and Andrew's opinions and that from other professionals who were involved in his care. As I have already mentioned I felt very much supported and knew that if I had any worries or concerns I could contact the CDC and make an appointment. On one occasion I met with the paediatrician by myself to talk through my concerns and worries. This was a very helpful experience for me especially as I was new to the world of autism. The paediatrician was also the professional who referred Tom to other services for help.

Firstly Tom was referred to the early year's speech and language team or SALT, who are also based at the CDC. We were put in touch with a lovely therapist who over the two years before Tom started school worked with Tom both at home, nursery and then preschool. She would visit Tom once a month rotating from home to preschool setting. She worked very closely with myself and staff and would devise targets that we would work towards. Therefore both I and preschool staff would be working towards the same targets, these involved lots of play. For example when playing with the toy farm we would involve Tom in the play by getting him to name the animals and to interact with them. For example, 'Tom, can you feed the horse?' and 'Tom can you put the cow on the tractor?' We also did a lot of turn taking games (this is something that Tom still struggles with) such as taking it in turns to play snap or to roll a ball. We certainly had a lot of fun and in the early days we could involve Stephen in the play activities which were fantastic. Making Tom do things he didn't want to do though did create frustration and meltdowns, something that was difficult to watch at first but for Tom to progress and learn he had to learn these social skills and is still learning today, he has made wonderful progress though. The meltdowns became less severe and less frequent and he started to look forward to the sessions. When we first started working with the SALT team we were lucky if Tom managed two minutes of structured play, as he would not sit and engage, whereas towards the end of the two years he was coping much better and would have a good session lasting up to thirty minutes. He has made such wonderful progress.

As already mentioned Tom was referred by the paediatrician to the child psychology service and my husband and I did have two appointments with a wonderful clinical psychologist regarding Tom's challenging behaviour. However although the appointments were very useful in giving us advice and strategies to use with Tom she never actually saw Tom as they were 'mini appointments' as the waiting list was very long. Something that is common for a lot of families I feel. However Tom and I did get several appointments eventually but at this time Tom's needs had changed. His challenging behaviour was less challenging and we now had problems regarding his separation from myself and this was causing problems with the preschool drop off as well as at home. Therefore the clinical psychologist was able to observe Tom and give some practical advice on ways in which we could better help him with this transition, something that we are still working towards today. There are unfortunately no easy solutions. After doing lots of research I found that separation anxiety is very common in children who are on the autistic spectrum.

When Tom turned two years of age we noticed that his stools (poo's) were becoming increasingly looser, frequent and foul smelling. He would pass four to six loose stools a day. This was causing great distress to Tom and therefore greater stress within the household; we had done some reading and had read about how replacing cow's milk for soya milk could help with this. Tom would drink around four hundred mils a day of cow's milk, so we decided that switching to soya milk would be very easy and would be a good start. We did this with guidance from our health visitor. Tom would not and still does not eat cheese or yogurts (although occasionally he will eat soya yogurt) so it was only really the milk that we had to substitute. Anyway after switching to soya milk we did see a slight improvement and then decided that we needed further advice about Tom being on a gluten free diet. We had read many books and sought advice on the NAS website and it seemed that there were many benefits including changes in bowel habit, concentration and behaviour that made it worth investigating. On one of our clinic visits I mentioned that we had changed Tom's milk from cows to soya and that we had seen a slight improvement. I then asked about the benefits of a gluten free (GF) diet and it was then that we were referred to the paediatric dietician. This was over six months ago. I had three visits in total. The first visit was for him to meet Tom and to chat about ways in which we could help him. This visit was an absolute disaster as Tom did not like being in a strange environment, it was at the local hospital, and he tried to escape from the room and then proceeded to throw anything he could grab his hands on. Luckily the dietician was very sympathetic and we decided that we were not going to achieve anything with Tom being so distressed. Once we had left the clinic room and Tom was seated in the play area, he then became a lot calmer and we were able to have a quick ten minute discussion in which he suggested that I try to find gluten free cereals (Tom's favourite foods being Cheerios and Cornflakes) and bread and see how we got on. He felt that if we were able to substitute Tom's favourite foods for GF ones then it would be well worth trying. On the following visit, which was a month later I went by myself while Tom was at preschool. We had found GF Cheerios and Cornflakes and luckily Tom really liked them. We had also found GF part baked bread which Tom enjoyed. Over the course of the month we saw an improvement with his bowel motions in that they became less frequent and more formed. From giving this information to the dietician it was decided that we should put Tom on a trial of a GF diet for a total of three months and see if his bowels continued to improve. He also hoped that we may see an improvement with regards to his behaviour as he had met many parents of children on the autistic spectrum who had observed remarkable positive changes in their child's behaviour in that they became calmer and exhibited less challenging behaviour. Well, even though I had read several books on the benefits of a GF and caesin free diet I was still very surprised to find out the huge positive impact it had, and still has on Tom's quality of life. We noticed that he became a lot calmer and was able to concentrate on task for a longer amount of time. His change in behaviour was also noted at preschool. I could not believe that a change in diet would have such a significant impact. With regards to making his diet exclusively GF this was relatively easy as his diet was and still is today very limited. Tom's diet consists mainly of cereals, bread, bananas, chicken nuggets, fish fingers, homemade chips, smiley faces, homemade GF sponge cake, GF spaghetti, breadsticks, soya milk, GF pancakes, fruit smoothies and eggy bread. Therefore the transition to GF was not too dramatic for us or for Tom. I do still worry about his diet though, even though the dietician has reassured me that his diet although limited is providing him with everything he needs. I would just like him to eat vegetables (I do give him peas and carrots, always cut the same way) but they remain untouched on his plate. He will not eat anything 'wet' or anything that is not consistent. I should be thankful though that he does eat, even though it may not be what I would prefer him to eat.

At our last clinic appointment with the paediatrician I discussed my concerns over Tom's reluctance to use a fork and spoon and to hold and draw with crayons and pencils. If he uses a spoon, which is very rarely, he tends to use it upside down and will either bite on it or simply drop the food from it into his mouth. He can use a fork, although held incorrectly, to stab at food but he prefers to then pull the food off and use his fingers. He will also use the fork to stab at other objects, such as the table and on occasions gently his face. He uses his fingers most of the time to eat even when I put soya milk on his Cheerios and this is a real concern. Because of this concern over his fine motor skills and related sensory issues it was felt a referral to the paediatric occupational therapist (OT) was indicated. We have only had one visit so far as the referral was only made recently but we are going to try and work on Tom's fine motor skills. This will include doing many activities and therapies such as encouraging Tom to draw basic shapes such as a line and circle to enable him to write letters. The OT on her first visit came to us at home but the plan once Tom starts school is for her to work with Tom once a month within the school setting. She also gave a very good idea of why Tom may struggle to put a spoon or fork into his mouth. This may be due to sensory sensitivities and that by getting him to chew on a dry toothbrush before eating may help to desensitise him.

So as you can appreciate there are many professionals who are involved in the care and diagnosis of your child. To begin with this may seem a frightening process and for me at first it almost felt as though I was handing over control to them, somehow I felt less powerful. However I soon realised the importance of my roll (and that of Andrew's too) in the diagnostic process. Never underestimate the power and knowledge that you have as a parent in being able to access and implement care in order to help your child.

Siblings

'Siblings of autistic children', just this phrase evokes all kinds of feelings and images of how young children deal with having a sibling who is on the autistic spectrum and of how us, as parents, try to support our other child with these feelings. This indeed is a very sensitive area. I can only describe what I do to try and support Stephen. When I started to do research and find out how siblings could be effected and ways in which I as a parent could help I was very much surprised to find out just how much help and support was out there for young siblings.

Stephen was only sixteen months old when Tom was born so they are very close in age. Stephen is now five and a half and Tom four. I find this to be a good thing. They do play well together in that Stephen invents games and Tom plays along, this mainly involves lots of running and high activity levels, especially running around the garden and jumping on the trampoline. However they do enjoy playing with the trains and cars together. Of course they fight as brothers do but on the whole are good friends, Tom is fond of saying "Stephen my best friend" and Stephen says the same of Tom.

We have always been open and honest with Stephen about Tom's additional needs and he knows that Tom is autistic. To help me with explaining Tom's autism and why Tom acted in certain ways I bought the book 'My Brother is Different' (2000), by Louise Gorrod. This was in the summer of 2011 when Stephen was four and a half. It really helped in explaining why Tom is different and without this book I am not sure if I would have got across what autism is and how it affects Tom in such a clear way for a four year old to understand. Stephen is now very knowledgeable and is forever telling people that Tom is autistic and that he helps him. Although this is a positive thing in that it shows that Stephen cares for and is very protective of him this is something that does concern me as well and in which I worry and feel guilty about. I do not want Stephen to feel that he has to care for Tom. I do not want him to become a carer. These feelings of Stephen's surfaced the other week when I was chatting to him about Tom and how he would be starting school. Stephen said 'don't worry mum, i will look after him' to which I replied that he did not need to worry about Tom as the teachers would all be looking after him. He then replied with' no mum, I worry about him, he is always on my mind, even when I can't see him'. This hit me hard, I didn't realise that this was how he felt. I have never asked him to look after Tom but this is something that he instinctively feels about his brother in that he has to take care of him. He is such a caring little boy and has a lovely nature that I do worry about what the future holds for him in having a brother who is 'different' and what implications this brings. I believe I am not alone in thinking this. Therefore I am forever finding out information and help that is available for siblings so that I am better informed and able to help Stephen access services in the future as well as gaining more information myself. It is important to remember that siblings need support as much as their parents.

I am very fortunate in that Stephen goes to AOK in the holidays with Tom and while there he is able to mix with other children who have additional needs as well as their brothers and sisters. This is a really healthy environment for him to be in and I am so happy that we can all access this service, especially as he gets older. He is only five but I am very aware that as he gets older he will need a support network of his own and be able to speak to his peers who are in similar situations. I started to find out what information was available and what support groups there were in preparation for the future and I was pleasantly surprised with what I found.

The NAS was the first website that I went to and I found a whole section dedicated to siblings who have ASD's. Firstly there is a reading list especially for younger sisters and brothers that I have found helpful. This is where I read the review of the book 'My Brother is Different' and knew it would be the perfect book to explain Tom's disability. The NAS also talk about the importance of children talking to their parents about the feelings that they have about their brother or sister with additional needs.

I often talk to Stephen about Tom and how he is feeling. This is very important especially if we have had a challenging day with him as this must have an impact upon him. What is really impressive though is that the NAS use simplified language to explain the triad of impairment (difficulty with social interaction, communication and imaginative play) and how this affects their sibling and why they behave the way that they do. To be honest I found it useful reading myself. It will help me with explaining to Stephen as he gets older and has better understanding.

We often try and give Stephen time with either myself or Andrew. Often at the weekend I will take Stephen into town to his favourite museum or to a cafe while Andrew has Tom and once a week Andrew takes Stephen swimming while I have Tom. This gives him a much needed break and some time for just him. I do find that when looking after the two boys I do have to concentrate more on Tom, especially when out and about due to safety reasons. I always feel guilty about this but I have no other choice, therefore time with just Stephen is very much needed as he gets all of my attention. It is hard sometimes to remember that he is only five as he seems much older. While traveling on the train the other week with the boys (we had been out as a treat to soft play) I got chatting to a lovely lady who worked with young children on the autistic spectrum. She made a comment that really struck home, that brothers and sisters of autistic children seem to grow up faster as they have more responsibility. I agree with this viewpoint but at the same time feel incredibly guilty about it.

Personal space is also very important I feel. The boys have their own bedrooms and often Stephen will go up to play in his room, we know when he does this that he needs some quiet time and we are respectful of this. It is something that I do myself; I often go and hide in the kitchen! What I really do resent and have most guilty feelings over is that we are limited to what things we can do as a family. This is due to many factors for example such as avoiding busy and noisy places, safety and facilities. However on the positive side there are many places we can go to as a family and these will be discussed in the chapter ' Going Out and About',

While exploring the support that siblings need it is very important that the role that grandparents play be discussed. For the very first time, this year as I write this book, Stephen has been away from home with both sets of grandparents, spending a week away from home with them. All of our extended family resides in the same area, about a one and a half hour drive from where we live. Therefore spending time with them has been a special treat for Stephen. I know that he is having the time of his life. He has been pond dipping, on steam trains and had copious amounts of ice cream so far. I am so happy that they are able to do this for him and that we have grandparents who are willing to help out.

Another concern that I have for Stephen is how he will be affected when Tom starts school in September 2012. Will he be teased as his brother is different? Will he have feelings of resentment towards his brother? How will his feelings change as he gets older? All of these questions go round and round in my head and I feel that all I can do is support Stephen and be there for him when he needs me. We are very fortunate in that the school do integrate all children with disabilities very well and there is a very caring ethos within the school for children with additional needs. In that I am thankful.

The NAS website was also were I found out about organisations that are solely for siblings; Barnardo's have several support groups around the country as well as Sibs who also hold details of support groups for child and adult siblings. I will be finding out what services are available locally for Stephen as I feel in the next few years he will need this type of support. As well as support groups help is also available on the web. The NAS helpline is also available to talk about concerns or any issues relating to siblings of children with autism. This is an excellent service. Other services that help inform and support siblings are Contact a Family, who have a very informative fact sheet especially for siblings. There are also online communities which can offer support such as SibsKids and autism_sibs. Stephen is too young at the moment to access these websites but as he gets older they will provide safe and helpful guidance and advice for him.

To conclude I just feel that the better informed and educated we are about what it must be like to have a brother or sister on the autistic spectrum, the better enabled we are to help and support them. Unless you have a sibling yourself who has a disability then you will never know what implications this will have on your life. We need to be empathetic towards their needs, worries and concerns. Most importantly siblings need a support network of their own and we can make this happen for them.

Going Out and About

   Going out anywhere with Tom always takes planning and a little thought, something that we are now getting better at. Maybe my stories of what we do when going out and the strategies we use may be of some help to you and give you some ideas to try out. Firstly I am going to talk about going into cafes and coffee shops. We do frequent these quite a lot and there are reasons for this. Firstly we have no family living nearby so I like to take the boys out for a treat and secondly I feel it is good for their social development, especially Tom's. He now loves going to the 'boy's coffee shop' for 'coffee juice' as he calls it, especially if he is with Stephen. He started going there from around the age of six months; this is a regular place that we visit. What is most important is that the cafe is not too busy or noisy. We usually manage this by going fairly early in the morning. We are usually at the 'boys' coffee shop' by ten a.m. By going to the same coffee shop at regular times we usually see the same customers and we now know the staff really well who in turn know our order off by heart! I always have a takeaway cup .They are also very understanding of Tom. Because this is somewhere that we visit regularly it does mean that Tom has several chairs that he likes to sit on. If his preferred chair is unavailable then he is usually happy to sit in his second choice, so far we have had no meltdowns there because he has several choices of where to sit. However when we go to the supermarket or 'car shop' as Tom likes to call it, and visit the cafe there, Tom particularly likes to sit on the couches but as there are only two of them these are usually occupied. Therefore visits there have to be very early so that he can have 'his couch'. On one occasion he tried to sit on a lady who was sat on his couch and attempted to push her off, this was highly embarrassing, but the lady thankfully was very kind and understanding once I had explained to her about Tom's difficulties. I do actually find this to be the case with most people, in that once they know about Tom's autism they are usually very understanding about his needs.

When going further afield and to unknown coffee shops and cafes this is when things become more difficult. As Tom is on a GF diet our choice of cafes can be limited. However I have on occasions explained to staff about his diet and autism and they have been happy for me to give Tom snacks from my 'snack bag' which usually consists of GF breadsticks and GF Cheerios'(thank goodness they exist otherwise life would be unbearable). However cafes are selling more and more gluten free items and as yet we have not struggled too much to find places to have a snack were Tom will be happy. I also have to check for escape routes and how safe the cafe is, this is especially true when new cafes open up in town and I always go by myself first to check them out. When out with Andrew and Tom last week we were having such a lovely time that we decided to stay and have some lunch. Andrew found a café, quickly looked inside and did a 'Tom check' before we took Tom inside just to assess how busy it was and how easy it would be for him to escape. Luckily it was fairly quiet, safe and served Tom's favourites, chips, so we were in luck. Another thing I would mention is that it is a good idea to always have money on you, not just debit or credit cards. I mention this because on one occasion when we were out we found a lovely little Tom friendly cafe but could not go in as we had no change and they did not accept cards. Luckily Tom was having a good day but if it had been one of his off days then not being able to stay in the cafe may have resulted in a huge meltdown and unhappy and stressed parents. The last thing I would like to mention is that apps on your mobile phone are absolutely fantastic for distracting your child and making the whole experience less stressful. I have an iPhone and it is loaded with many autism apps and general children's apps. This helps Tom when having to wait for food or drink as it helps to keep him busy and therefore means that I am able to finish a meal or drink as he will happily play on it(this is true most of the time). I just make sure that the volume is not too loud.

We have been to the cinema on several occasions although we have not been recently, the last time being a year ago, Tom does struggle once he is there. The films that are for his age group are usually too long, at least two hours in length, and we usually end up leaving after an hour.

The sound is also extremely loud, even with ear defenders on and I feel that Tom does struggle with this We did however enjoy the last film we went to see which was a Thomas the Tank Engine film, it was only on for an hour and on that occasion the sound was not as loud. The Odeon branch of cinemas have autism friendly screenings once a month in which noise levels are reduced, soft lighting is on throughout the film and customers are allowed to move around freely. You can also purchase a Cinema Exhibitors' Card (CEA) which can be used in any cinema. This entitles the carer to free admission when accompanying the cardholder, they are very easy to apply for, and I have one for Tom. They cost £5 for a year's membership.

At the beginning of the book I talked about how difficult our daily bus journey to nursery was but now thankfully Tom really enjoys riding on the bus. It will come as no surprise that we have to sit on the same seat every time. However as we always sit at the back of the bus this is usually not a problem. He will happily sit and look out of the window and I think that he enjoys the vibrations of the bus. A few months ago Andrew took Stephen to Edinburgh for the weekend and so therefore I had Tom at home. It was during this weekend that I decided to take Tom on a long bus journey to see how he would react; our usual bus journey only takes fifteen minutes so I wondered how he would cope for an hour? Well it was a total success; we had our snacks while sitting happily on the top deck of the bus. He absolutely loved it. It will be a trip that we will be making again.

As well as bus rides Tom loves going on the train, this is a real treat for him, especially if he is with Stephen. We often go on the train to a soft play centre located in the building of a train station. The journey takes around forty minutes and so far we have only had one incident. This was when we were sat at a table; Tom and Stephen were sat on either side looking out of the window. Unfortunately the seats and all the others in the carriage had been reserved so I knew at some point we would possibly have to move. Luckily there were only two stops. Anyway unfortunately a lady got on with two children and we were sat in their seats. Well as soon as I made attempts to try and move Tom he started to have a meltdown, there was no way he was going to sit happily elsewhere. I therefore had to explain about Tom's autism and once I had done so the lady was very sympathetic and understood completely and allowed us very kindly to sit there until we reached our stop. I will never forget her understanding and how kind she was to Tom, even though he tried to push her suitcase off the table, the table always has to be clear! Train rides though are usually an enjoyable experience for Tom. What I must add though is that I always use backpack reins when going on the train. The backpack I have for Tom Is in the shape of a cow and he loves to wear them. It also looks less obvious than standard reins.

A place that Tom loves to visit is the local museum in town. I used to take him as a small baby as it was lovely and quiet in there and I used to enjoy looking at the paintings. So it was a place that he was familiar with. We always take the same route when walking through the museum and Tom especially likes the model of a man sat in some stocks that he calls 'the naughty man'. The museum is now known rather amusingly as 'the naughty man' to all our friends. We also now know the staff very well and they know Tom by name, it is a lovely place to go to and I think that Tom feels calm there. Even better it is free!

Tom is now much happier in town as long as we don't go when it is extremely busy, before eleven a.m. seems to be the best time. He will happily walk along holding my hand but we do need to go into several shops just to go up the escalators and ride down in the lift. This is a compromise which I do not mind very much, it keeps him happy and I am able to buy a few things.

Tom loves playgrounds, as do all children, but again we have to check that the area is safe with no easy escape routes before he can play. When out last week with Andrew we found a lovely little playground by accident with locked gates, Tom had a fantastic time playing there.

I also want to quickly mention about trips to the hairdresser. We take Tom and Stephen together. Tom has been going for several years now after an unfortunate haircut that I gave him. He had a somewhat wobbly fringe. He does struggle when there though and usually comes out with comments such as, 'help, help, it's an emergency, I need to go to the hospital!' This however is very short lived and usually the promise of a 'coffee juice' makes it all better.

Tom really enjoys his visits to the farm. We are very lucky in that we have several farms near us but the one he likes best is Docket Park Farm. It is quite a large farm with a cafe, small play barn with bouncy castle, toddler area in a barn, outside play area and lots of ride on tractors and bikes. As well as all the fantastic animals including pigs, goats, lambs, donkeys, chickens and Tom's favourites the owls. Tom feels very safe there and is free to run about. What was lovely was that a few weeks back they held a fun day for the NAS and raised a lot of money for them. We all went and met up with other children and parent carers from AOK, we had a lovely day.

Lastly where Tom really likes to go is for a walk along the canal and then to a local cafe where he can sit outside and watch the trains pass by. We are very fortunate in that we live a short walk away from the canal. I always put his cow backpack reins on and am always armed with copious amounts of bread to feed the ducks. It is lovely to stroll along for a short while and it also has the added effect of tiring him out.

Therefore I would urge you to go out and have fun. You may run into difficulties but you cannot let this stop you. Plan ahead, go to places that you know well and are safe. Most importantly though enjoy yourself and your children.

Toilet Training

This for me has been the biggest challenge so far and as yet even though Tom is now aged four years and four months he is still in nappies. This is a growing concern for me, especially as Tom will be starting school soon. His continence needs will be dealt with at school so from that point of view it is not a huge concern but for myself I still struggle with the fact that I have a four year old who still wears nappies. I cannot help but think, 'what do other parents think? 'What will other children say?', 'do people think I am a lazy parent?'. This is certainly not the case. We have tried lots of ways in which to help Tom (of which I will describe) and I am still looking for help and resources. I just think that at this moment in time he is not ready developmentally. I am really hoping that in a year's time he will be out of nappies, or at least in the daytime.

So when and where did I start looking for help? I must be honest and say that I didn't even entertain the idea of starting toilet training until Tom turned three years of age. Stephen only took a week at the age of three to be dry and clean both in the day and at night, with the occasional accident, so I thought that three years of age would be a good starting point for Tom and that things would progress in much the same way although a little slower.

However life is never that easy. Firstly it was very difficult to even get Tom into the bathroom. No matter what I did he stubbornly refused to go in and sit on the toilet. He would also show no reactions to being wet or dirty, even when I put kitchen towel in his nappy. He would walk about quite happily with a very large and uncomfortable looking wet nappy and part of me thought that he probably liked the feeling. Perhaps the weight of the nappy made him feel secure; it was a nice feeling for him. Therefore I was at a stumbling block to begin with. So, at a complete loss I decided to find out what information was out there. As a starting point I started looking at the toilet training pages on the NAS website. (I knew that regular toilet training advice would be of no use to training a child with ASD).

The two strategies I used as a starting point, taken from the NAS website were to try and get Tom happy to be changed in the bathroom and for him to be happy and sitting on the toilet at nappy changing times. This in itself took a very long time to achieve. As a starting point to actually helping him recognise that the toilet is where we do 'wees' and 'poos' I decided to use a visual timetable. This was the best thing I ever did as it enabled Tom to understand the actual process and sequence of events when going to use the toilet. At this point I was not overly concerned about him doing anything in the toilet I just wanted him to be able to go through the process and be familiar with the sequence of events. For example that you go upstairs, pull down trousers, sit on the toilet and so on. I decided to make my own visual timetable with the use of Picto Selector. This is free software that you download onto your computer and which then allows you to make your own visual timetables. You can use their own images, add words and even add your own photographs. There are lots of other PECS (picture exchange communication system) out there for sale which would also be useful. I used their symbols which I printed out and arranged on a piece of A4 paper which I then laminated, I made two copies. One I placed on the wall in the bathroom and the other I kept downstairs for Tom to familiarise himself with. This was how I was able to get Tom to go upstairs, he would look at the timetable, read aloud all of the symbols and then walk upstairs with myself to the bathroom looking at the timetable in his hands. I remember the day that this first happened and felt such an achievement. I had got him happily up the stairs and into the bathroom, something very small a lot of people would say but for me this was a huge step and starting point for Tom. I also gave a copy of the visual timetable to preschool so that when changing his nappy there he was able to follow the visual clues as it was familiar to him and be able to sit on the toilet happily.

There was an abundance of useful information and resources regarding all things to do with toilet training on the NAS website. The main points being that you need to have a routine which is reinforced by the visual timetable so that the child's anxiety is reduced as they can see the sequence of events. Using the potty was also discussed and it was voiced that the introduction of the potty may be confusing to some children on the autistic spectrum because once established on the potty they then have to make the transition to the toilet. I therefore decided not to use the potty. This however was my own personal choice. I never used the potty with Stephen for this very reason and I also had images of Tom throwing a very full potty over his head if not in a particularly happy mood. What I also found interesting was that the whole toilet training process takes a very long time for some children on the autistic spectrum and that the process should be divided into small steps to make the whole toileting adventure more manageable. This was further explained in the publication 'One Step at a Time'. This publication is available via the PromoCon website and you purchase it as a CD-ROM, the cost for me at the time of purchase was £10. The CD-ROM comes with many printable resources including the book as mentioned, fact sheets and visual aids that can be used to make a 'toilet book'. I made a 'toilet book' for Tom using the images and found it to be very useful. Stephen would very proudly sit and read it to him. I have the book in his bookcase so that it is always available and we often read it together. You could however make your own toilet book using photographs or drawings. It needn't be expensive. All of the media on the CD-ROM is very flexible in the way that you use it. 'One Step at a Time' breaks the whole process down into five steps, starting at setting the scene and then progressing onto being dry at night time. It is very important that your child feels comfortable and safe when in the bathroom. We purchased a child toilet seat and a step stool so that Tom could sit on the toilet by himself and feel safe when sat there as his feet would be placed on the stool and not dangling mid-air. What I also thought was very useful was their checklists for charting were your child is in the progress that they are making and therefore what the next step will be. I urge you to have a look at the website. One other point to add is that they have continence nurse advisers on their helpline. I used this several times to ask for advice and to find out what services were available locally.

Community forums are an extremely valuable resource for discussing all things 'toilet' related, I was constantly prowling for posts regarding all matters toilet related and I definitely sought solace in other parents tales that there nearly school age children were still in nappies. It made me feel like I was not alone. I also got much wanted advice and tips.

As well as seeking advice on the internet I also sought advice locally from a variety of different resources. Firstly I went to my health visitor and asked for advice. She was very helpful and supportive and referred Tom to a continence nurse specialist at my request. We did have one appointment with her but with discussions afterwards with my health visitor we came to the conclusion that Tom was not ready developmentally to be toilet trained. I was given some strategies to try out including using visual aids, which I was already using, changing in the toilet, again what we were already doing, but when I tried Tom without nappies for several days he was just urinating everywhere other than in the toilet! Hopefully once at school I will be able to access the services of the school nurse and gain help and support from her. The other help I received was from other parents. Just chatting to them about Tom made me feel less of a bad parent and that it was 'normal' for autistic children to take longer in being able to use the toilet. Even though I had read this in many different formats it still made me feel better to actually hear it out loud.

From all of the literature that I had read it suggested that the child needed to be able to sit on the toilet for at least two minutes for toilet training to be successful. I had succeeded in enabling Tom to sit on the toilet for a few seconds but I had therefore to think of ways in which to entice him to sit there for longer. Again I looked for advice on the internet and asked friends for any ideas and I was not disappointed. The ideas ranged from using a toy bag in the bathroom, reading a book, putting colourful pictures on the walls, having a sticker chart on the toilet door and playing music. I did over time try these ideas and they had very little effect. The two ideas I tried that did work and are working today are blowing bubbles and playing with the apps on my IPhone. Firstly blowing bubbles seems to be very effective. I simply tell Tom that if he sits on the toilet we can have bubbles and he usually cooperates. If the prospect of blowing bubbles does not excite him then I say that he can play on my phone. I have many apps on my phone as previously mentioned, but I find that I have to constantly add new ones and rotate them to keep Tom interested. Thankfully there are lots of free apps and I tend to use these. Recently over the holidays we found that due to the change in routine Tom regressed with his toileting. He would no longer walk up the stairs and would throw himself on the floor and refuse to move. This would often result in him throwing things when we tried to move him. Looking back this now seems quite funny but at the time I found it very frustrating, heart breaking and dismaying to watch. He made me so angry, we had made such good progress and even though I knew the reason for his behaviour it still made it no less difficult to observe and understand. In the end I refused to let him win and we continued to change him in the bathroom. This then resulted in both Andrew and I having to carry a usually noncompliant Tom up the stairs. Over the weeks he did become more cooperative and his behaviour less challenging. What I used to help get us back into the routine we previously had was to find new apps and in particular I found a free potty training app which included 'Cars 2' stickers which is one of his favourite films. This thankfully helped us get back on track. What is still difficult though is the morning and night time nappy change. He refuses to sit on the toilet first thing in the morning as he wants to go straight downstairs and before bed he just wants to climb into bed. I do however try and get him to sit on the toilet before having his shower and sometimes I am successful. I have even tried letting him see Stephen doing a 'wee' on the toilet, something that Stephen is very proud of, he will do a running commentary in his best teacher voice while using the toilet much to my amusement, but this sadly has not encouraged Tom.

I am hopeful that once Tom starts school and we are receiving extra help for him regarding his continence that we may be able to implement a toileting routine both at home and school. Perhaps with this and the fact that he will be a little bit older may result in him using the toilet and allow us to say goodbye to nappies for ever. I am hopeful.

In the Home

Your home is where you should feel safe, were you are free to be yourself, to relax and have fun. This is how it should be for everyone. Having a child on the autistic spectrum does add stress to home life but you can still have a happy and relaxing home. You just need to adapt your way of thinking and that of your home to accommodate the needs of your child and the changing needs of the family as a whole. We live in an average sized house with three bedrooms, one bathroom, separate toilet room, a back garden that is fully enclosed and safe, an open plan living room, conservatory, small hall and kitchen. We also have outbuildings that we use for storage. I will take you on a virtual tour of the house to give you a sense of what life is like for us at home and perhaps give you ideas to try out.

Firstly there is the issue of safety regarding the front door. I always have the door locked and the keys removed from the door. This is because Tom can now reach the keys and it would be very easy for him to open the door and to escape. Even though we do not live on a busy main road this fills me with fear as he could go anywhere. He has very little sense of danger and he can run very fast.

We have a small hallway and this area is safe, we just keep our coats and shoes there, Tom is only here when we are about to go out. Leading from the hall is a staircase which is quite steep and the room attached to the hallway is the living room. When Tom was younger he was safe from climbing the stairs as he could not get out of the living room as the door handle was too high for him to reach. From around the age of two onwards he really struggled in going up the stairs, his foot used to slip and he would place two feet on each step, therefore I would always walk up with him. Going down the stairs posed a bigger danger. He would almost try and launch himself down the stairs and on one occasion he tried to jump down, luckily I was able to stop him as I was with him. I therefore taught him from a young age, as I did with Stephen, to go down the stairs on his bottom, we called this 'whee bump'. He would still require me to be with him and to hold his hand but at least he was safe. At this time when the stairs proved to be a danger for Tom we had a stairgate placed at the top of the stairs. This at least ensured that once upstairs Tom was safe. We still use it now at night time. The stairs are now a much safer place for Tom. He walks up them slowly and carefully and he knows to walk slowly down. This he has learned over time. Some children though will have more complex needs with navigating stairs and this is where input from OT's and physiotherapists are needed.

The living room posed other problems. Although not very large it is an open space and Tom loved and still loves to run. He will run very fast up and down the room. We therefore had to move anything that was breakable. Also because Tom can throw things when in a meltdown it is best that we have no expensive ornaments or decorations that could be broken. We also have no coffee tables, the reason being that they could be easily knocked over and Tom would just climb and jump off them. We have a little sensory area in the living room for Tom and this helps Tom to be relaxed and calm but also allows myself to be calm and relaxed in the same room. It is amazing what a mat, cushions and small sensory toys can do. As Tom gets older and starts school full time we will probably have a smaller sensory area in the living room and create a sensory space in his bedroom. We will probably do this over time so that he gradually adjusts to his new space. We also bought a projector with the help of The Family Fund and by projecting soothing and colourful images onto his bedroom wall this should help create a lovely relaxing space for him. This is difficult to do at the moment as he is safer downstairs were I can keep an eye on him but over time I will need to give him more space and independence and this will be one way of being able to achieve this. As well as having his sensory area we also have a PlayStation for him to play on. This however was second hand as we refused to pay for a new one knowing that it would probably be thrown. It has been thrown on many occasions, less so now and luckily so far it has survived. Tom and Stephen also have their own bookcase with cushions and beanbag. Again this created a space for Tom in which he can sit happily and look at his books. I do find that by having actual areas were Tom can sit that this does help to reduce his activity levels and keep him calmer. On one occasion I tried to move his sensory area to another part of the room, I was having one of my many room changes, but Tom did not approve of this and moved everything back where it originally was. Therefore I would say to keep things consistent and to not move them once established, it does make life easier.

Related to this are structure and the use of routine and visual timetables. I do like my routine and would have one even if Tom did not have additional needs. However having a routine is very important for reducing Tom's anxiety and therefore helping to create a happier household. We always do the same morning routine in that Tom wakes up, comes into our bedroom and then we go downstairs. Then Tom has a drink of milk. If I tried to deviate from this sequence of events then problems would arise. We have a similar routine at bed time. We tidy the living room, and then have a shower, go downstairs for calm time (easier said than done at times), milk then bed. Again by doing this routine Tom knows that he is getting ready for bed and sleep. I have to say that I do love my routines. To help with this we also use Pecs cards. These are pictures, symbols or photographs that are used to help with communication. I use homemade ones as part of a visual timetable to help explain the main activities of the day. We actually purchased a talking timetable from TTS on their website. They have a good selection of sensory items and aids for children with special needs. The talking timetable can be mounted on the wall or simply placed on a flat surface. It has six slots were the picture cards can be placed. For example the first card will show a picture of clothes, then the second a photograph of a bowl of Cheerios followed by a photograph of a bus. You can then record your voice, very simply by talking into the microphone. So for example I would say about the pictures, 'Tom getting dressed', and then 'Tom having his cereal' followed by 'Tom going on the bus'. Using the visual timetable proves to be very effective with Tom even though he is verbal. Many children on the autistic spectrum are visual learners and I do find personally that if Tom can see an image as well as I talking about it then this does improve his understanding. You do not need to buy a talking timetable though, you could simply make one and we do use a homemade one a well. Once you have all of your photos or pictures I would laminate them so that they last longer. Then you attach Velcro (the type that comes with the two sides you need to stick together) to the back of the card and then put a strip of Velcro onto a piece of card and attach it to that. This way the cards are easily added and removed on a day to day basis. It is very cheap to make as well. Adding structure to the day certainly helps us as a family.

The living room is also were Tom's laptop lives. He can therefore play on it while we can watch him. We do have to set time limits though as he would be on it all day if he could. I try and limit his use to no longer than forty five minutes and to help with this I usually give Tom a countdown when it is nearing the end of his time on it. This is usually in the form of ten minutes, five minutes, two minutes, one minute and finish now. This on the whole seems to work very well. If I was to say to Tom, 'turn the computer off now Tom' without any warning he would most certainly have a meltdown. You can also use visual timers such as egg timers and sand timers to help with this. We also have a 'car box' in the living room filled with cars. This opens up into a mat and Tom will quite happily lie on the floor surrounded by them. When bored with his cars he will then often ask for his trains. We have a box containing a wooden train track as well as a 'take and play' set. This is fantastic when visiting family as all you do is open it up and the track is ready to play with.

Leading on from the back of the living room is the kitchen. When Tom was younger this proved a problematic room. He could easily enter the kitchen and so we very quickly added a safety gate to the door. This did enable me at first to cook in the kitchen and for Tom to keep safe. However he very quickly learned to open the gate and would simply run into the kitchen and either crash into myself or throw himself onto the floor. He did not like the physical barrier of the gate and having one caused more problems than not having one. We therefore removed the gate and kept the door shut. Over a long period of time he began to understand when it was safe to enter the kitchen. I just had to be even more vigilant with Tom when cooking and on most occasions when by myself with the children I would prepare food in advance when Tom was napping so that minimal cooking was needed later on in the day. The kitchen though is also a fun place. This is where we play with play dough and play foam. Tom also likes to sit at the kitchen table and listen to the radio, his favourite channels being Planet Rock and Radio Four, while helping to make cakes as he likes to crack the eggs. Things are much better now thankfully.

At the back of the house we have a small conservatory which is where we eat our meals. Tom particularly likes it in there as there are many windows which look out onto the garden. Sitting and eating a meal for Tom can be quite a stressful experience at times, as already discussed. I do find though that If Tom is seated at the table with a favourite book or one of his birds then he will sit for a short while. We have a cross trainer in the conservatory or as the boys affectionately name it the 'Og Pog', and what usually happens is that Tom will eat some of his meal and then have a ride on it. This is hilarious to watch, and then he will sit back at the table to resume his meal. To an outsider this behaviour must seem very strange as well as naughty but it allows Tom to eat at the table and over time hopefully he will be able to sit for longer.

Tom's bedroom at the moment is very basic. He associates his bedroom for sleeping and where he goes if he has been naughty for 'time out'. This room is the safest place for him when having a meltdown and he soon calms in there. There is nothing really for him to throw other than his stuffed toys and bears and he calms down relatively quickly. Tom is now in a normal bed but he was in a cot bed until around the age of three. Part of this reason was that he felt secure in this bed and another was that he was safe. He very soon settled into his big bed though and we had no major problems, I think because we waited until he was ready.

Tom also loves the bathroom. As already mentioned he loves the routine of getting ready for bed and winding down. He loves having a shower and then being able to play with his favourite toys, the boats and ducks. He also enjoys the feeling of the water on his back and he loves to lie in it. It is very calming for him as well as being lots of fun. The only thing that we really struggled with was getting him to brush his teeth. This has been an on-going battle that has only very recently been overcome. To begin with I would give Tom the toothbrush to play with so that he would get used to the feeling in his mouth. Then I gradually added some toothpaste. He would put the brush in his mouth and chew on it but not really brush with it. However I was happy that at least he was accepting of it. He would happily do this at bath time of an evening but would not cooperate of a morning. I even tried putting a photograph of his toothbrush on his visual timetable but this had no effect. Anyway as I say quite recently I was looking on my phone for new free apps for Tom and found one called 'Talking Ginger', this is a cat who repeats what you say which is great for language development in itself but more importantly it features the cat brushing its teeth for two minutes accompanied by music. There is also a progress bar at the bottom of the screen. So with the help of this app Tom has now successfully been brushing his teeth every morning!

Lastly I want to talk about the garden. We are very lucky in that we have a fair sized garden for the boys to play in, grow fruit and veg in and explore. Tom loves to run and he is able to do this outside. He usually runs all around the outside of the garden in a huge circle. He loves doing this, even when it is raining. We have a slide in the garden as well as a trampoline which both boys enjoy immensely. If Tom can get out into the garden every day we certainly see an improvement in his behaviour as he is able to burn off energy and gain the sensory stimulation that he craves. It is far better for him to run around outside rather than up and down the living room.I also encourage Tom to use pavement chalks outside as he is very reluctant to use pencils or crayons to draw with and I have been successful on some occasions. Generally though I just end up chalking with Stephen myself which actually is a lot of fun.

The home therefore should be a happy place where you spend time together. Our house at the end of the day is usually very messy and I always feel that this shows we have had fun and generally a good time. If you can have fun with your children at home then I feel that this is a real achievement and something to celebrate! You may just have to adapt your home slightly so that you can achieve this.

Education

Getting the help and support you need at an early years setting (nursery or preschool) is absolutely vital. Early intervention is paramount in ensuring that your child has the best possible start regarding their learning, socialisation and understanding of the world. A positive experience at preschool will better prepare them for their journey to school. I will take you on the journey we had with Tom regarding his early year's education, the help that we received and the help we sought for preparing him for school.

Tom attended nursery from the age of two, he went for two mornings a week, each session lasted three hours and it was identified after a few months of him being there that he was struggling and not coping within the nursery setting. Tom's difficulties included, speech and language delay, unable to follow instructions, simply wanting to follow his own agenda, poor concentration levels and difficulties in sharing. He therefore was identified as needing help within the nursery setting and it was decided that the process for getting help from the educational professionals specialising in early years should be started as soon as possible. This was the Early Years SEN (Special Educational Needs) team. This was the first step towards Tom receiving the help and support he needed with regards to his learning needs. The whole processes for acquiring specialist help and input in an early years setting and then subsequently school is not a simple one. I could write a whole book on this topic alone. I will therefore only give a brief outline of the help that Tom received at preschool and the process we followed for attaining a statement of educational needs for school. At the moment the government are proposing a change to the way children with additional needs and disabilities are supported in schools. They produced a consultation document entitled, 'Support and aspiration: A new approach to special educational needs and disability' (2011). The government are proposing that by 2014, all children with SEN will have an 'education, care and health plan'. This will replace statements of educational needs. A draft legislation has now been published 'Reform on provision for children and young people with Special Educational Needs' (2012).Therefore a lot of changes are taking place regarding education but the point I want to get across is that children on the autistic spectrum can get extra support, and should get extra support and help both in the early years setting and at school.

When Tom started nursery we were very fortunate in that my outreach worker was able to give help and support to nursery staff. Tom had been referred to the Early Years SEN Panel but was not able to access support and the services of the Early Years SEN teachers until the term after his third birthday. This resulted in him receiving help when he started preschool in September 2011, a full academic year before starting school.

However we were able to access the services of Portage for two terms before Tom started preschool. Portage is a home teaching service for preschool children who have two or more developmental delays. A Higher Level Teaching Assistant (HLTA) visits on a weekly basis within the home and 'play's with the child'. We had a fantastic lady who worked with us and both Stephen and Tom looked forward to her visits. She would bring a big bag filled with toys and we would do things such as playing 'Pop up Pirate' and matching picture cards. Stephen was included in the play as well and Tom was encouraged to take turns and follow simple instructions, two things that he struggled with. At the end of the session we would have a story. I still really miss these visits, even after over a year.

When Tom started his preschool year at the age of three years and five months he was supported in the setting firstly by a Special Educational Needs Coordinator (SENCo). This was a fantastic member of staff who understood Tom's difficulties and disability and who worked with him on a one to one basis. He was also supported by an early years inclusion teacher and a HLTA. He was awarded a set amount of hours each term and the teachers would observe Tom and then work with the preschool staff in setting targets and using strategies to help support him. For example Tom found it very difficult when entering preschool as he did not want to be separated from myself. To help with this we decided to use a visual support system in the form of photographs showing Tom entering the building with me, taking his coat off, entering the room, saying goodbye to me and then a photograph of myself walking home and then returning to preschool. This was so Tom could see the sequence of events and therefore hopefully having the effect of reducing his anxiety levels. This did work for a short time. The preschool also made a safe sensory space for Tom, consisting of cushions and beanbags. This was a place where Tom could go if he was feeling overwhelmed and overstimulated and indeed if he was feeling tired. This proved to be very effective.

While at preschool I started to have conversations with the preschool manager, the SENCo, and specialist early years teachers about how Tom would be supported once he started school. It was agreed that he would need specialist help and support at school and that he would need a statutory assessment to assess his needs. This is where the local authority asks your views as well as those of the early years setting, your paediatrician and those of an educational psychologist. We also had input from the SALT. This process can in itself seem quite complicated especially as you have to submit a written statement yourself, which is a parental advice form. All of the other professionals involved also have to submit their own reports. The more information you submit the better as this will help to give a clearer picture of your child and their needs. You know your child best and remember that the Special Educational Needs and Disability Officer reading the information and who is responsible for issuing a statement of educational needs will never have met your child. I just want to mention here that the involvement of an educational psychologist might seem a bit daunting, but from my own experience I found it to be very enlightening. The psychologist visited Tom at both preschool and then at our home. She was a lovely lady and explained in great detail to me the whole SEN process. She was excellent with Tom and totally understood him and his needs. At one point in our discussion he tried to get into her handbag and then when he had had enough he got hold of her coat and said 'lady, go now'. We just had to laugh. Once all of the information has been received the local authority then decided to issue a statement of educational needs which is a legal document. The statement will detail your child's disability and all SEN. For example with Tom it is stated that he needs help with personal care and toileting as he is still in nappies. It will also detail the help your child will receive in school and the hours dedicated to this. For example that your child requires a full time HLTA, due to their complex needs. The whole process of acquiring a statement of educational needs is indeed very complex but as already stated the whole process is going to be reformed by 2014. More information about SEN can be found in the booklet,' Special Educational Needs (SEN) - A guide for parents and carers' (2008).

I just want to mention briefly before discussing the ways in which we helped prepare Tom for school, about the excellent Parent Partnership Service. This is a statutory service that provides impartial help and support to parent carers of children with SEN. This service is also free. Their services include supporting parent carers when attending meetings, giving information and advice about how SEN are assessed and give help to patent carers if they are not happy with a decision that has been made regarding their child's SEN. I myself used this service when going through the process of Tom gaining a statement and I found the service to be extremely helpful and supportive.

How did we help prepare Tom for school? For any child, making the step from preschool to school is a huge one. There is a longer day, lunchtime, structures and rules and many changes including a bigger building, lots of new children and lots of new adults. For a child on the autistic spectrum this is a huge challenge due to many changes in structure and routine with lots of new sensory information to process. Therefore the transition to school for children on the autistic spectrum in itself comprises of many challenges and difficulties. In the case of Tom these difficulties would include having to cope with lots of children in a busy classroom, having to adapt to new surroundings and people he had never met. To help prepare Tom for these changes it was decided that I should make a 'talking school photo book' for Tom to read over the summer holidays. This book consisted of many photographs taken of the school building, classrooms, teachers, teaching assistant, hall, library and even the toilet. This was to help familiarise Tom with the school building and teachers before starting school with the aim of helping to reduce his anxiety. When looking at a picture in the photo book you can also press a button on the page and a pre-recorded voice explains the picture. So for example with the photograph of the toilet, Stephen recorded 'this is the toilet'. Stephen and I had lots of fun making the book and I was very happy that I could involve him with this task for his brother. However it felt very strange going round the school photographing the teachers! Hopefully the book will have a positive impact on Tom.

The school also had several settling in sessions. For these sessions parents left their children with the Reception class teachers for an hour. However after liaison with the school it was decided that Tom's SENCo at preschool would assist Tom in these sessions as he would be with a known and trusted adult therefore enabling him to better enjoy the experience. He did enjoy his settling in sessions even though he did try and escape from the classroom several times, he did not get very far though.

I also had several meetings with the Head teacher and Tom's future teacher in the build up to the summer holidays so as to give them advice about strategies I use at home as well as discussing Tom's needs when in school. I am very fortunate in that Tom will be assigned a full time teaching assistant when starting school.

Therefore to conclude preschool children can receive extra help and support in their early years setting. At the moment there are many changes taking place with regards to SEN and at this time I am unsure if these changes will be for the best, only time will tell. Be proactive in the decision making process regarding your child's education, you know them best. The school and local education authority have to listen to you. Good luck.

Final Thoughts

I hope that you have enjoyed reading about Tom and my family and the journey that we have been on. Looking back it is very difficult to remember those early days as we have made such progress. This happens in little steps though until you suddenly realise one day that things are different, they creep up on you. Never give up, keep on talking to people and asking questions, do your research, get out there and meet other parents with children on the spectrum. Do not isolate yourself. Be the best advocate you can be for your child and help them achieve the best that they possibly can.

Who knows what the future holds for Tom or indeed for any of us. We survived the early years as a family and I am sure we can face any other problems and difficulties that come our way. The next few years will come with their own challenges and difficulties but I am forever learning and adapting to new situations and changes and therefore feel as if I will be prepared, also having an excellent support network helps with this. It's also difficult for me to say goodbye to those early years, I now will have two children in Primary School. How did that happen? The years seem to have passed by so quickly.

All I want to say is that I have enjoyed having the boys at home and playing and having fun with them. But Tom is now reaching the next chapter in his life and I and Andrew have to do our upmost in helping prepare him for these changes. Enjoy your special child. Even though autism can seem to dominate your life at times(clinic appointments, reading books and research, coping with challenging behaviour) do not let it stop you from enjoying this special time with them. Listen to your child as well, I often think that I know what is best for Tom and try and make him adapt to my ideas of what I think is right but often it is best to listen to your child, put yourself in their world and adapt to them. This will help you tremendously. Also remember yourself; you need to look after yourself in order to look after your child.

Finally I really hope that you have found this book useful and that you now do not feel so alone. Have fun, make sensory dens and go out for coffee and cake. Enjoy life and most importantly laugh, a lot.

Useful Information

Websites

National Autistic Society

Free Helpline 0808 800 4104

www.autism.org.uk

Contact a Family

Free Helpline 0808 8083555

www.cafamily.org

Sensory Toy Warehouse

www.sensorytoywarehouse.com/

TTS (Educational Supplies) Where I bought Tom's visual talking timetable.

0800 318686 (early years resource)

www.tts-group.co.uk

The Cinema Exhibitors' Association Card (CEA Card)

0151 348 8020

http://www.cinemauk.org.uk/cea-card/

RADAR Key

This is a key to access public toilets. Keys cost £3.50

0207 250 3222

Email radar@radar.org.uk

Information about DLA and Carer's Allowance

www.direct.gov.uk

Cerebra

Help and information line 08003281159

www.cerebra.org.uk

Family Fund

01904658085

www.familyfund.org.uk

PromoCon

0161 6078219

www.disabledliving.co.uk/PromoCon

Unique Kidz and Co

01524 874047

www.uniquekidzandco.org.uk

Email info@uniquekidzandco.org.uk

SEN Assist

www.senassist.com

ASD Friendly

www.asdfriendly.org

AuKids magazine

www.aukids.co.uk

Email aukidsmag@gmail.com

This is a positive parenting magazine for parents of young children on the autism spectrum. It offers practical, upbeat ideas and advice over 12 full colour pages designed to inspire and entertain. It is run by parent and journalist Debby Elley, whose twin sons have autism, and speech and language therapist Tori Houghton, who has specialised in autism for 12 years and also runs a support agency for autistic children.

To subscribe to the quarterly magazine, go to www.aukids.co.uk or write to AuKids magazine, PO Box 259, Cheadle, Cheshire SK8 9BE enclosing a cheque for £10 payable to AuKids magazine with your name and address written on the reverse.

For an extra £5, subscribers can take advantage of a package that includes AuKids' Starter's Special, a collection of their most popular features designed for parents who are new to autism.

Starters' Specials are also available to support groups and diagnosis clinics free of charge.

Talk about autism

www.talkaboutautism.org.uk

National Parent Partnership Network

Find your local parent Partnership service

http://www.parentpartnership.org.uk/find_your_local_pps.aspx

Boomerang Multi-Sensory Play Centre

www.boomerangcentre.co.uk

Special Educational Needs (SEN) A Guide for Parents and Carers

Available in print/online

0845 60 555 60

www.teachernet.gov.uk/publications

Support and aspiration: A new approach to special educational needs and disability (2011)

www.education.gov.uk/publications/eOrderingDownload/Green-Paper-SEN.pdf

Reform on provision for children and young people with Special Educational Needs' (2012)

http://www.official-documents.gov.uk/document/cm84/8438/8438.pdf

SEN Magazine

www.senmagazine.co.uk

Information for Parents. Autistic spectrum disorders (ASD's) and related conditions.

0845 6022260 ref ES12

www.education.gov.uk/publications/eOrderingDownload/ES12-2010.pdf

Sibs UK Charity

01535 645453

www.sibs.org.

Barnardo's

0208 5508822

www.barnardos.org.uk

Space Play Centre

http://www.thespacecentre.org

SibKids

www.siblingsupport.org/connect

Autism_sibs

http://health.groups.yahoo.com/group/autism_sibs/

Docker Park Farm

01524221331

www.dockerparkfarm.co.uk

ERIC

Helpline 08453708008

www.eric.org.uk

Portage

www.portage.org.uk

JJ's Sensory Play Centre

www.jjsplaycentre.co.uk

Safe play centre

www.spclip.co.uk

The Sensory Processing Disorder Website (has useful articles, resources and links).

www.spdnetwork.org

Experience books (personalised books for children in the autistic spectrum)

www.experiencebooks.co.uk

Picto Selector

www.pecsforall.com

Facebook groups

Parents and children with disabilities support group Morecambe PCDS

www.facebook.com/groups/131419196945588/

North Lancashire Directions Group Parent Carer Network NLDG

www.facebook.com/groups/NorthLancsDirectionsGroup/

Super Sensory Information Buddies – Sefton

www.facebook.com/groups/226835244094115/

North West - Act Now For Autism

www.facebook.com/groups/ACTNOWforAutismLiverpool/

Apps for IPhone / IPad (Tom's favourite ones)

Little writer- the tracing app (free)

Splingo's Language Universe (£1.99)

Talking Tom (free)

If you're happy and you know it (free)

Lego 4+App (free)

Lego Duplo Jams (free)

Little Fox Music Box (£1.99)

Kinectimals Lite (free)

Old McDonald Had a Farm (free)

TocaTrain (free)

Rockford's Rock Opera 1(free)

Angry Birds Space (69p)

CSR Racing (free)

Phonics Awareness, 1st Grade (free)

Books

Al-Ghani , Ki. & Kenward, L. (2011) From Home to School with Autism: How to Make Inclusion a Success.London: Jessica Kingsley Publishers.

Ariel, C.N. (2005) Voices from the Spectrum: Parents, Grandparents, Siblings, People with Autism, and Professionals Share Their Wisdom. London: Jessica Kingsley Publishers.

Batts, B (2010) Ready, Set, Potty!: Toilet Training for Children with Autism and Other Developmental Disorders. London: Jessica Kingsley Publishers.

Bleach, F. (2001) Everybody is Different: A Book for Young People Who Have Brothers or Sisters with Autism. London: The National Autistic Society.

Bogdashina, O. (2003) Sensory Perceptual Issues in Autism: Different Sensory Experiences - Different Perceptual Worlds. London: Jessica Kingsley Publishers.

Breton, L.M. (2001) Diet Intervention and Autism: Implementing the Gluten Free and Casein Free Diet for Autistic Children and Adults - A Practical Guide for Parents. London: Jessica Kingsley Publishers.

Coucouvanis, J.A. (2008) The Potty Journey: Guide to Toilet Training Children with Special Needs, Including Autism and Related Disorders. New York: Autism Asperger Publishing Co.

Cumine, V. (2009) Autism in the Early Years: A Practical Guide (Resource Materials for Teachers). London: Routledge.

Daly, M. (2012) With a Little Help from my Friends. Liverpool: Michelle Daly.

Derbyshire, G.J. (2010) Stand Up for Autism: A Boy, a Dog, and a Prescription for Laughter London: Jessica Kingsley Publishers.

Fairfoot, E. (2004) My Special Brother Rory. London: The National Autistic Society.

Gorrod, L. (2000) My Brother is Different. London: The National Autistic Society.

Griffin, M. (2012) It's Haircut Time! How One Little Boy Overcomes His Fear of Haircuts. Arlington: U.S.A.

Johnson, J. (2010) Siblings: The Autism Spectrum through Our Eyes. London: Jessica Kingsley Publishers.

Koutsis, A. (2006) What About Me? The Autism Survival Guide for Kids. Victoria, Australia: Wanting Heights School

Kranowitz, C.S. (1998) The Out-Of-Sync Child. New York: G.P. Pulman's Sons.

Kubler-Ross, E. (1973) On Death and Dying. London: Routledge

Legge, B. (2008) Can't Eat, Won't Eat: Dietary Difficulties and Autistic Spectrum Disorders: Dietary Difficulties and the Autism Spectrum. London: Jessica Kingsley Publishers.

Larson Kid, S. (2010) My Child Has Autism, Now What? 10 Steps to Get You Started. London: Jessica Kingsley Publishers.

Leicestershire County Council Education Department & Fosse Health Trust. (1998) Autism: How to Help Your Young Child. London: The National Autistic Society.

Moor, J. (2008) Playing, Laughing and Learning with Children on the Autism Spectrum: A Practical Resource of Play Ideas for Parents and Carers. London: Jessica Kingsley Publishers.

Overton, J. (2003) Snapshots of Autism: A Family Album. London: Jessica Kingsley Publishers.

Siegel, B. (2007) Helping Children with Autism Learn: Treatment Approaches for Parents and Professionals. New York: OUP USA

Tamsin Hunter, S. (2006) My Sister is Different. London: The National Autistic Society.

Welton, J. (2004) Can I Tell You about Asperger's Syndrome? A Guide for Family and Friends. London: Jessica Kingsley Publishers.

Winslet, K. (2012) The Golden Hat: Talking Back to Autism. New York: Simon and Schuster.

Woodcock, L. (2009) Managing Family Meltdown: The Low Arousal Approach and Autism. London: Jessica Kingsley Publishers.

Yack, E., Aquila, P, & Sutton, S. (2003) 2nd ed. Building Bridges Through Sensory Integration: Therapy for Children with Autism and other Pervasive Developmental Disorders. Arlington. U.S.A.

Gluten free cakes

Banana cake

8oz GF self-raising flour

6oz caster sugar

4oz butter

2 eggs

2 big bananas or 3 small bananas (over ripe is best).

1 tsp. xanthan gum

Put all ingredients in a bowl and mix together. Once all mixed place in a loaf tin, I use a silicone one as the cake is easily removed. Cook for 40 minutes at 180 degrees Celsius / gas mark 4, and then reduce to 150 degrees Celsius / gas mark 2 for thirty minutes. Allow to cool then remove from the tin and place on a wire rack.

Chocolate chip muffins

3 eggs

6oz self-raising flour

6oz butter

6oz caster sugar

200g chocolate chips

Set oven at 200 degrees Celsius / gas mark 6. Place all ingredients in bowl and mix well. Place in individual muffin cases (I use silicone ones). Cook for 20 minutes.

Play dough Recipe

2 cups flour

2 cups water

1 cup salt

1 tbs oil

1 tbs cream of tarter

few drops food colouring

(Optional glitter)

Place water, oil and food colouring into a pan; add glitter now if you are using it. Add the flour, cream of tartar and salt. Stir well, turn on the heat to a low setting and heat gently, stirring all the time. Continue until it thickens and is shaped into a ball. Remove from pan and allow to cool before kneading.

Snow Storm Shaker in a Bottle

Find an empty plastic clear bottle and fill with water till three quarters full. Add glitter and small plastic stars and snowflakes. Replace the lid and secure with colourful tape. This is very easy and cheap to make but very effective as a sensory toy.

Printed in Great Britain
by Amazon.co.uk, Ltd.,
Marston Gate.